HAL•LEONARD®

BASS
PLAY-ALONG

AUDIO
ACCESS
INCLUDED

PLAYBACK+
ed • Pitch • Balance • Loop

Play 8 Songs with Tab and Sound-alike Audio Tracks

T0039774

To access audio visit:
www.halleonard.com/mylibrary

Enter Code
3387-7987-3355-0854

Cover photo provided by Photofest

ISBN 978-1-4584-1494-6

EXCLUSIVELY DISTRIBUTED BY

HAL•LEONARD®

Visit Hal Leonard Online at
www.halleonard.com

CONTENTS

Bass Notation Legend

Bass music can be notated two different ways: on a *musical staff,* and in *tablature.*

THE MUSICAL STAFF shows pitches and rhythms and is divided by bar lines into measures. Pitches are named after the first seven letters of the alphabet.

TABLATURE graphically represents the bass fingerboard. Each horizontal line represents a string, and each number represents a fret.

Notes:

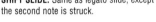

3rd string, open   2nd string, 2nd fret   1st & 2nd strings open, played together

HAMMER-ON: Strike the first (lower) note with one finger, then sound the higher note (on the same string) with another finger by fretting it without picking.

PULL-OFF: Place both fingers on the notes to be sounded. Strike the first note and without picking, pull the finger off to sound the second (lower) note.

LEGATO SLIDE: Strike the first note and then slide the same fret-hand finger up or down to the second note. The second note is not struck.

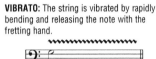

SHIFT SLIDE: Same as legato slide, except the second note is struck.

TRILL: Very rapidly alternate between the notes indicated by continuously hammering on and pulling off.

TREMOLO PICKING: The note is picked as rapidly and continuously as possible.

VIBRATO: The string is vibrated by rapidly bending and releasing the note with the fretting hand.

SHAKE: Using one finger, rapidly alternate between two notes on one string by sliding either a half-step above or below.

NATURAL HARMONIC: Strike the note while the fret hand lightly touches the string directly over the fret indicated.

MUFFLED STRINGS: A percussive sound is produced by laying the fret hand across the string(s) without depressing them and striking them with the pick hand.

BEND: Strike the note and bend up the interval shown.

BEND AND RELEASE: Strike the note and bend up as indicated, then release back to the original note. Only the first note is struck.

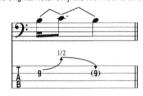

RIGHT-HAND TAP: Hammer ("tap") the fret indicated with the "pick-hand" index or middle finger and pull off to the note fretted by the fret hand.

LEFT-HAND TAP: Hammer ("tap") the fret indicated with the "fret-hand" index or middle finger.

SLAP: Strike ("slap") string with right-hand thumb.

POP: Snap ("pop") string with right-hand index or middle finger.

Additional Musical Definitions

(accent)	• Accentuate note (play it louder).
(accent)	• Accentuate note with great intensity.
(staccato)	• Play the note short.
	• Downstroke
V	• Upstroke
D.S. al Coda	• Go back to the sign (𝄋), then play until the measure marked "***To Coda***," then skip to the section labelled "**Coda**."

D.C. al Fine	• Go back to the beginning of the song and play until the measure marked "***Fine***" (end).
Bass Fig.	• Label used to recall a recurring pattern.
Fill	• Label used to identify a brief melodic figure which is to be inserted into the arrangement.
tacet	• Instrument is silent (drops out).
	• Repeat measures between signs.
	• When a repeated section has different endings, play the first ending only the first time and the second ending only the second time.

NOTE: Tablature numbers in parentheses mean:
1. The note is being sustained over a system (note in standard notation is tied), or
2. The note is sustained, but a new articulation (such as a hammer-on, pull-off, slide or vibrato) begins, or
3. The note is a barely audible "ghost" note (note in standard notation is also in parentheses).

Back in Black

Words and Music by Angus Young, Malcolm Young and Brian Johnson

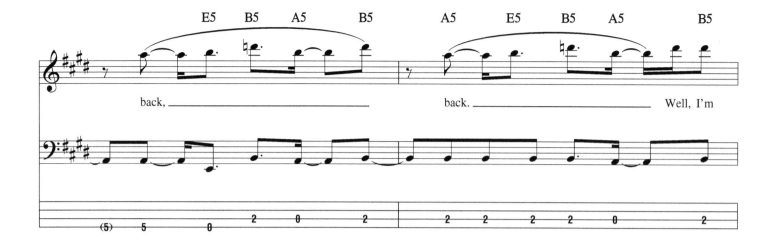

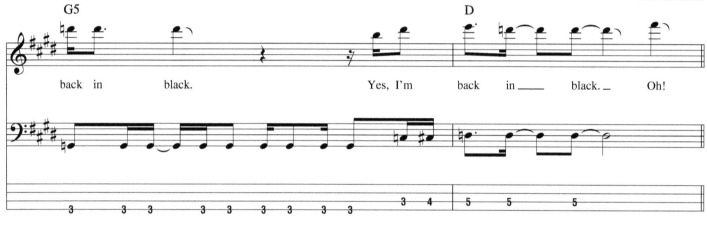

D.S. al Coda

 Coda

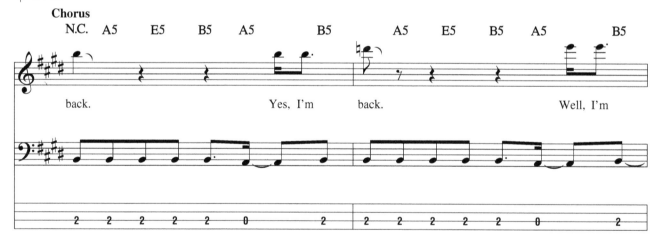

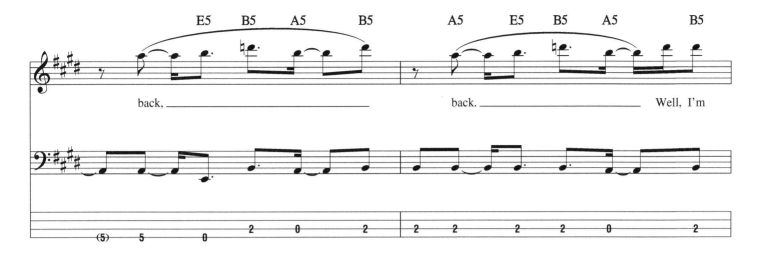

back, _____ back. _____ Well, I'm

back in black. Yes, I'm back in ____ black. _ Oh!

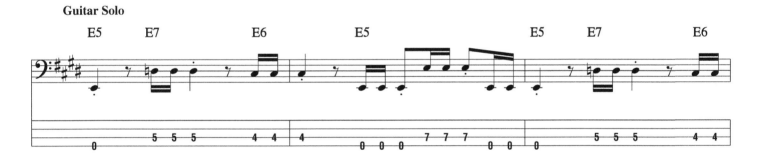

Guitar Solo

Chorus

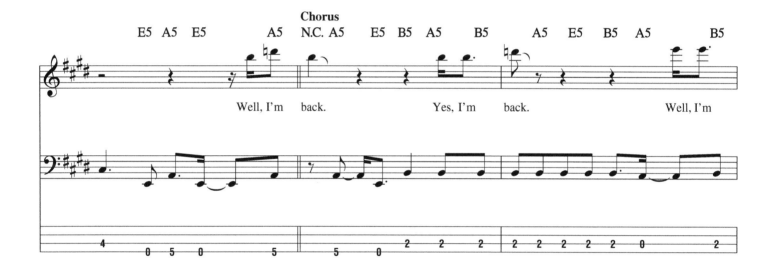

Well, I'm   back.   Yes, I'm   back.   Well, I'm

back.   Yes, I'm   back.   Well, I'm   back,

back. _____ Well, I'm back in   black.   Yes, I'm back in ___ black. _ Oh!

Interlude

N.C.(E5)

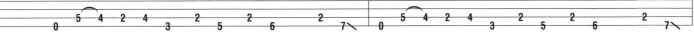

(A5)

(E5)

Well, I'm

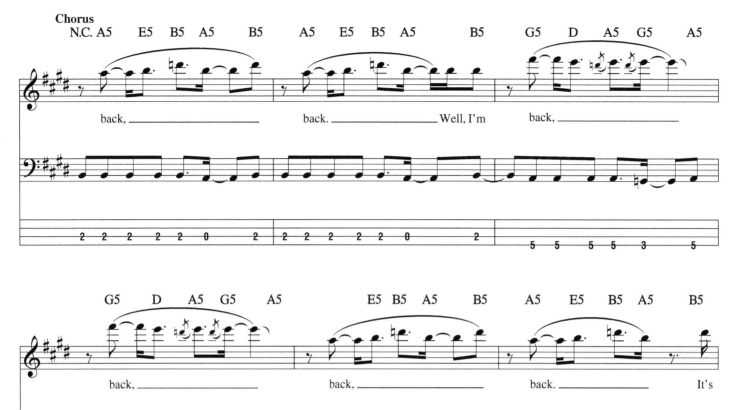

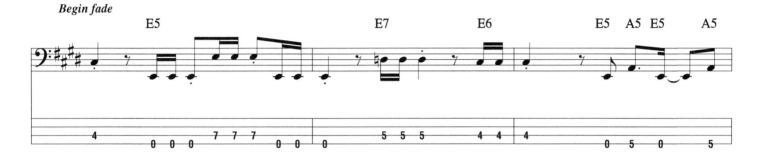

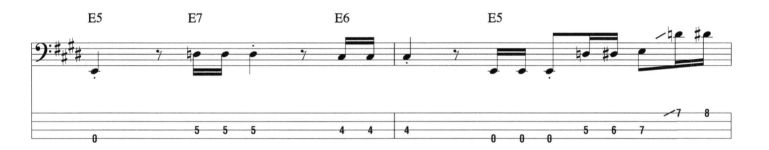

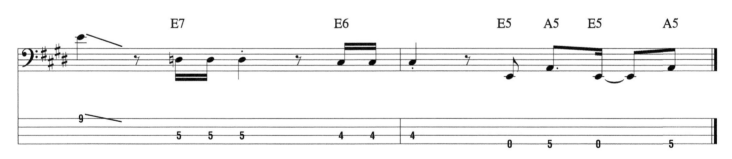

Additional Lyrics

2. Back in the back of a Cadillac.
Number one with a bullet, I'm a power pack.
Yes, I'm in the band, with the gang.
They got to catch me if they want me to hang
'Cause I'm back on the track,
And I'm beatin' the flack.
Nobody's gonna get me on another rap.
So look at me now, I'm just a makin' my pay.
Don't try to push your luck, just get outta my way.

Dirty Deeds Done Dirt Cheap

Words and Music by Angus Young, Malcolm Young and Bon Scott

Intro
Moderate Blues Rock ♩ = 134

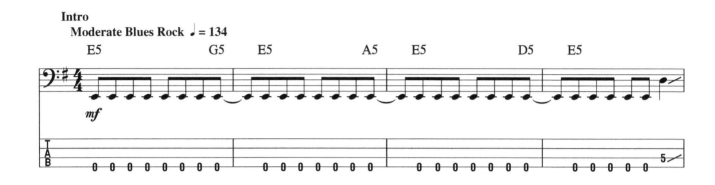

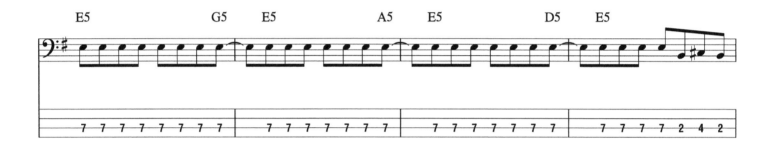

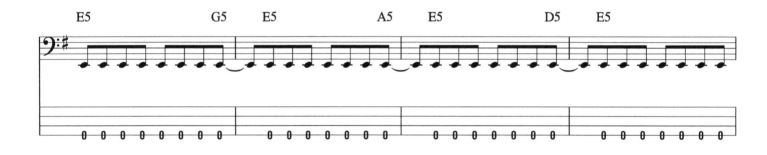

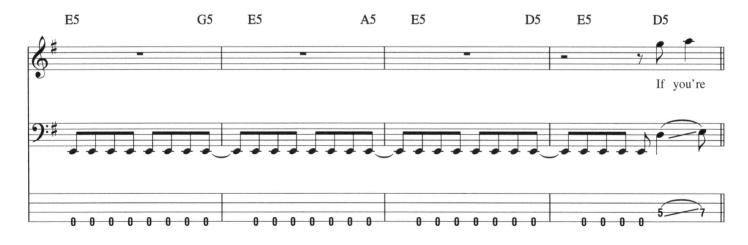

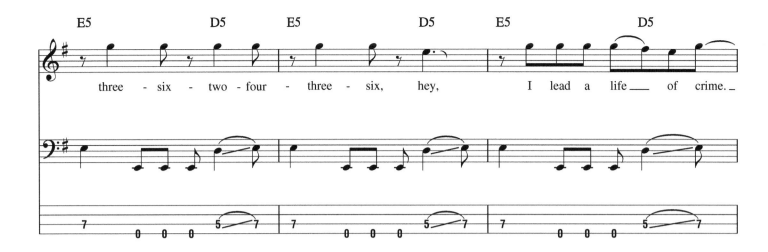

three - six - two - four - three - six, hey, I lead a life ___ of crime. ___

Chorus

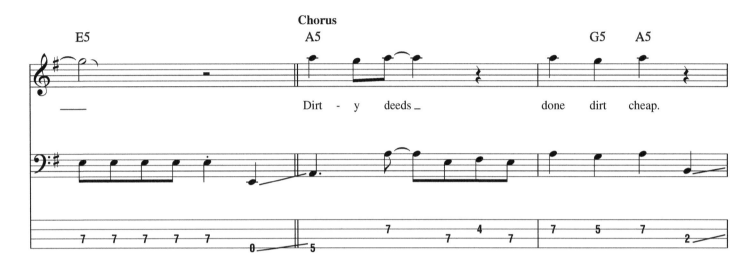

___ Dirt - y deeds ___ done dirt cheap.

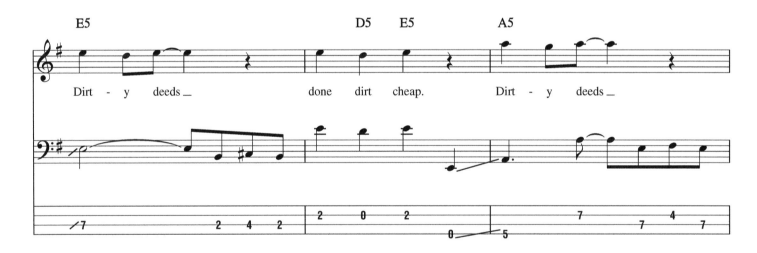

Dirt - y deeds ___ done dirt cheap. Dirt - y deeds ___

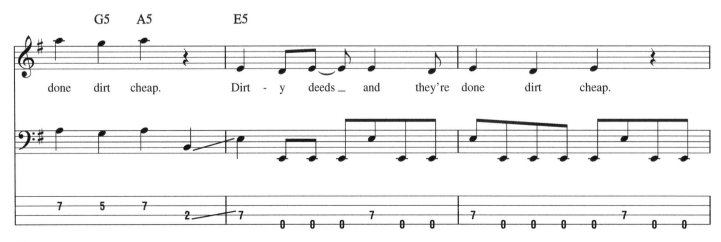

done dirt cheap. Dirt - y deeds ___ and they're done dirt cheap.

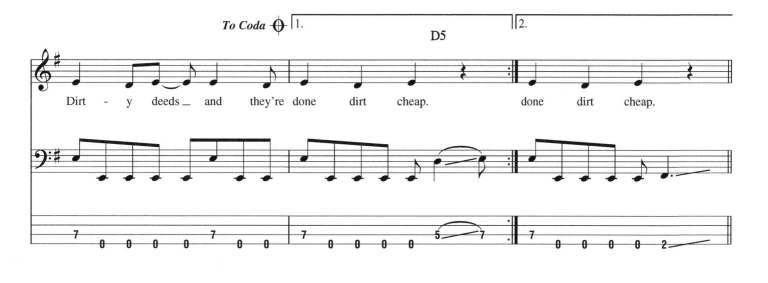

Guitar Solo

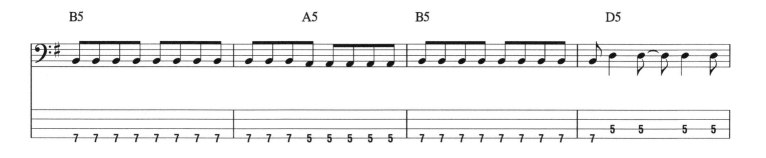

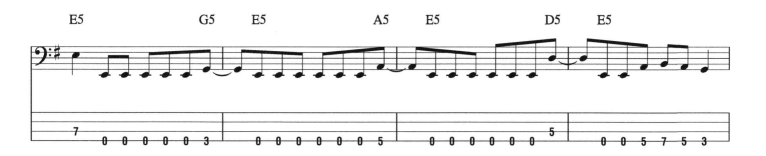

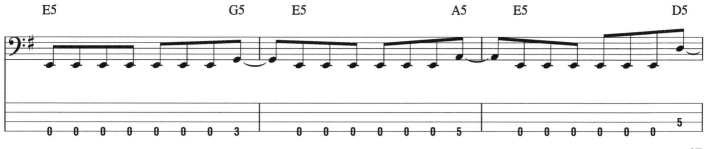

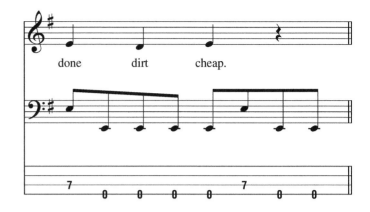

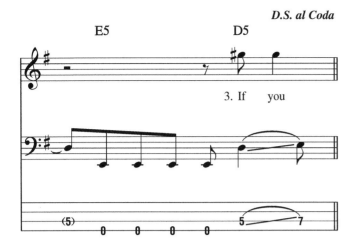

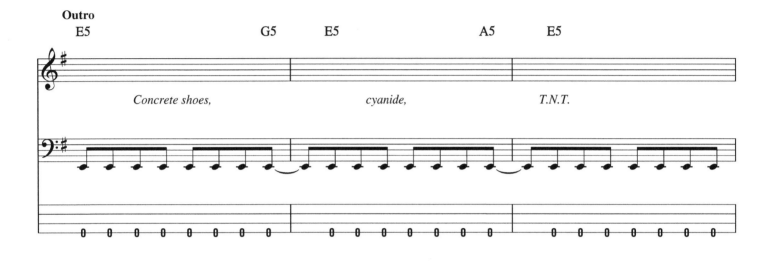

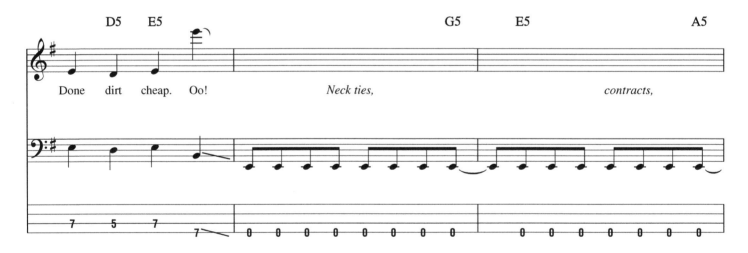

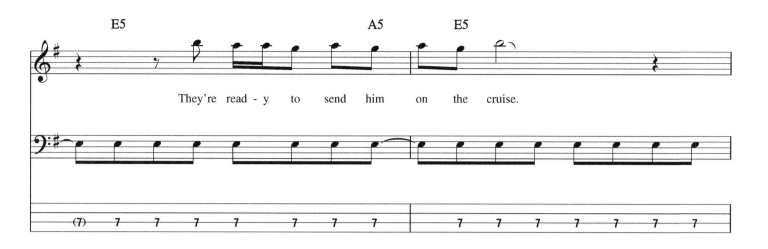

They're read-y to send him on the cruise.

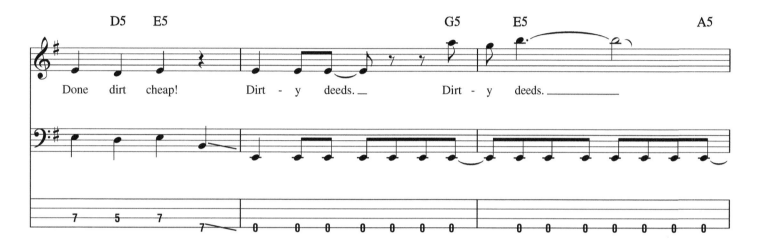

Done dirt cheap! Dirt - y deeds. __ Dirt - y deeds. _____

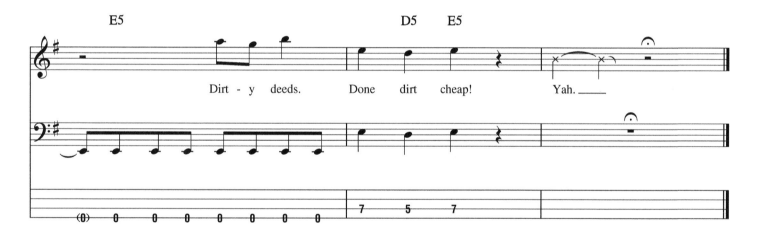

Dirt - y deeds. Done dirt cheap! Yah. _____

Additional Lyrics

2. You got problems in your life of love,
   You got a broken heart.
   He's double-dealin' with your best friend,
   That's when the teardrops start, fella.
   Pick up the phone,
   I'm here alone, or make a social call.
   Come right in, forget about him,
   We'll have ourselves a ball. Hey!

3. If you got a lady and you want her gone
   But you ain't got the guts.
   She keeps nagging at you night and day,
   Enough to drive you nuts.
   Pick up the phone, leave her alone,
   It's time you made a stand.
   For a fee, I'm happy to be
   Your back door man. Hey!

For Those About to Rock (We Salute You)

Words and Music by Angus Young, Malcolm Young and Brian Johnson

Intro
Moderate Rock ♩ = 127

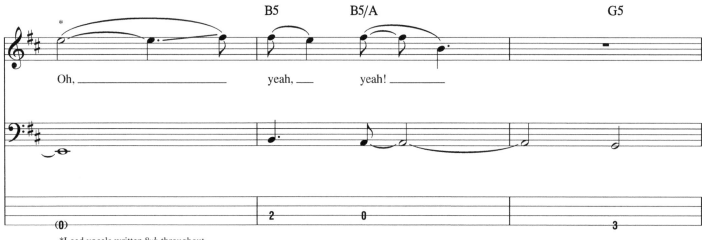

*Lead vocals written *8vb* throughout.

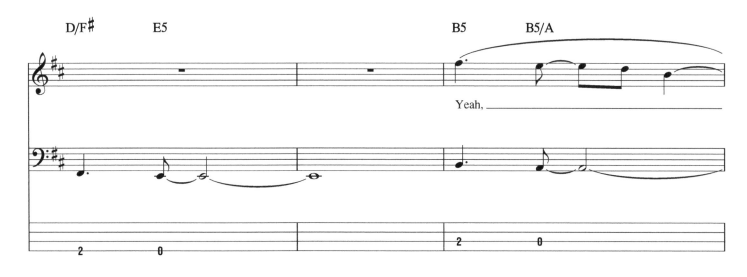

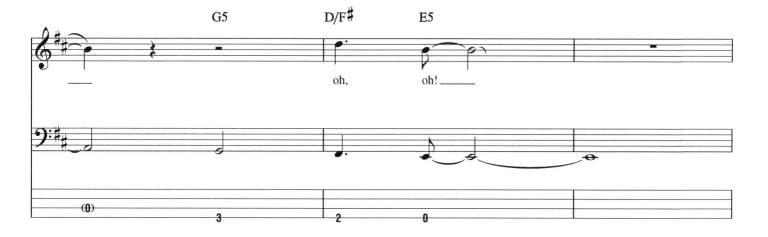

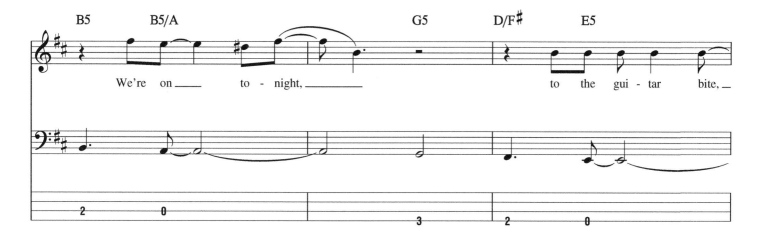

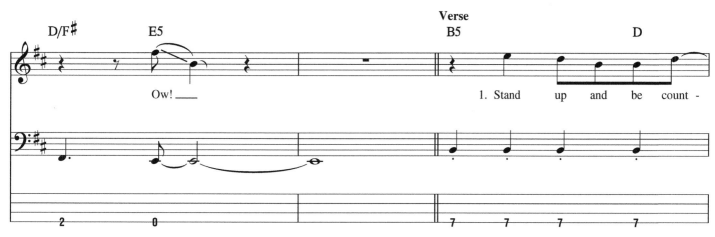

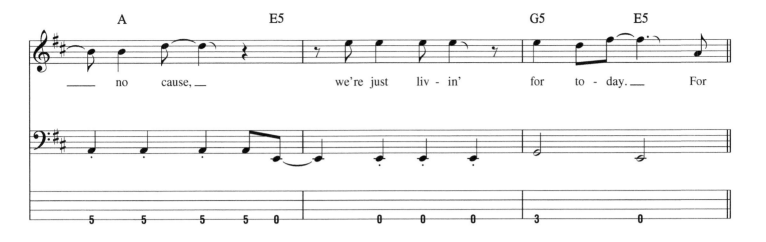

no cause, we're just livin' for to-day. For

Chorus

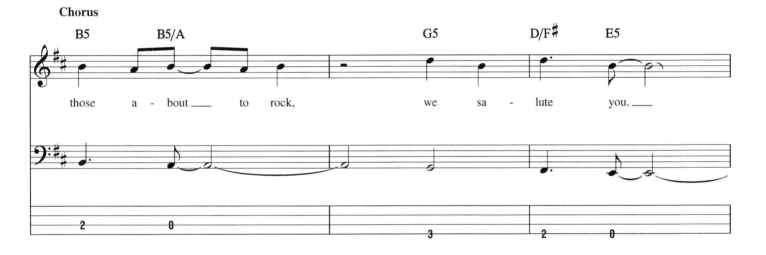

those a-bout to rock, we sa-lute you.

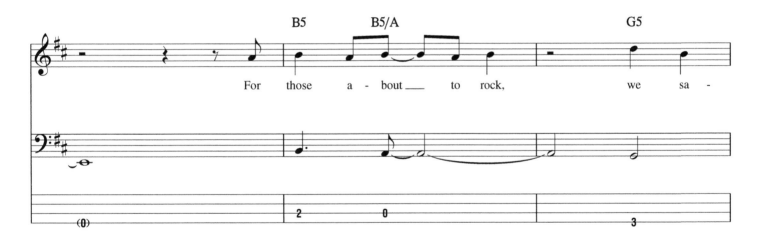

For those a-bout to rock, we sa-

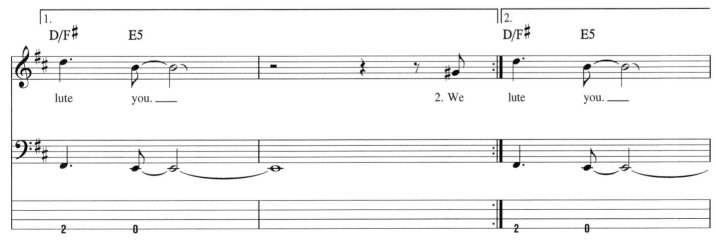

lute you. 2. We lute you.

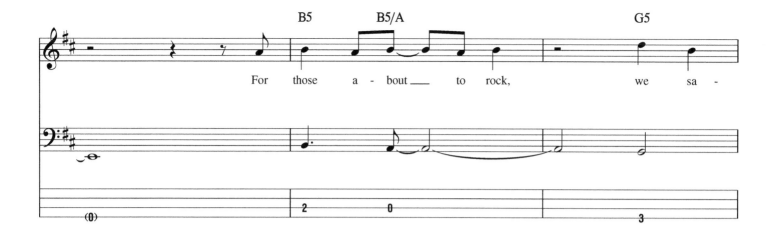

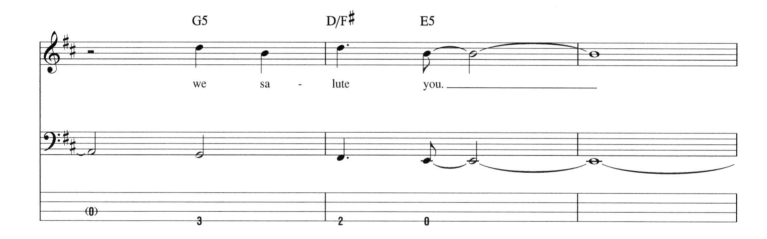

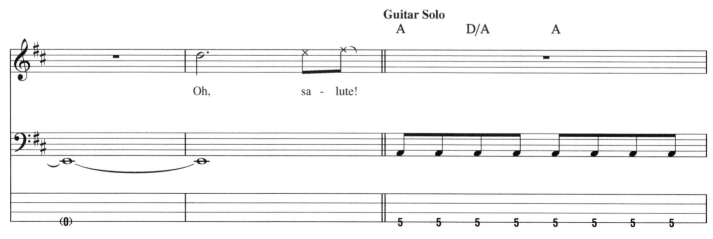

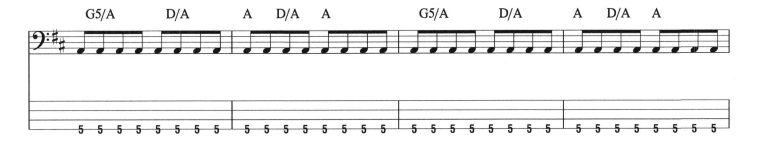

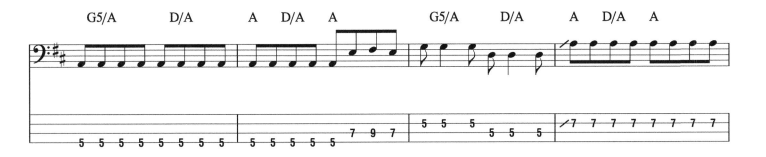

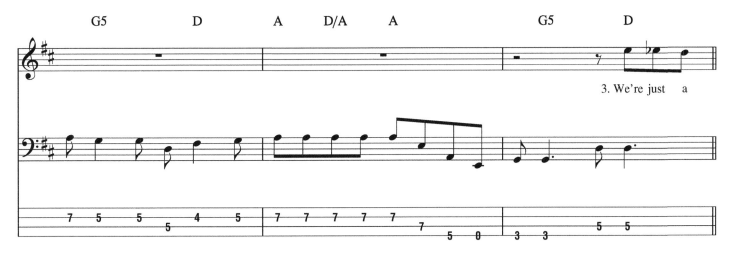

3. We're just a

Verse

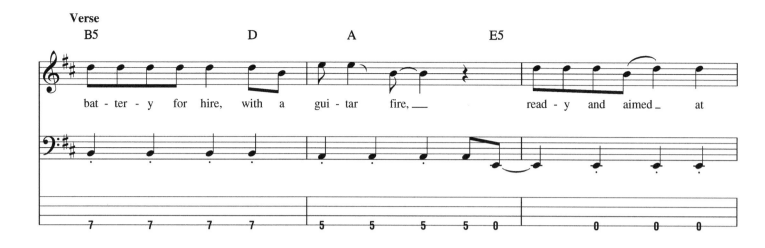

bat - ter - y for hire, with a gui - tar fire, ___ read - y and aimed ___ at

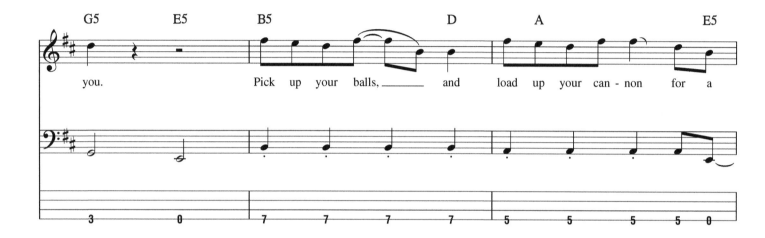

you. Pick up your balls, ___ and load up your can - non for a

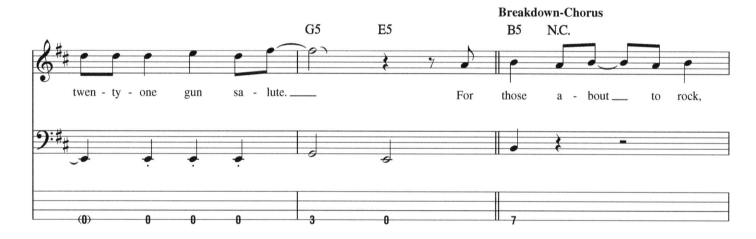

twen - ty - one gun sa - lute. ___ For those a - bout ___ to rock,

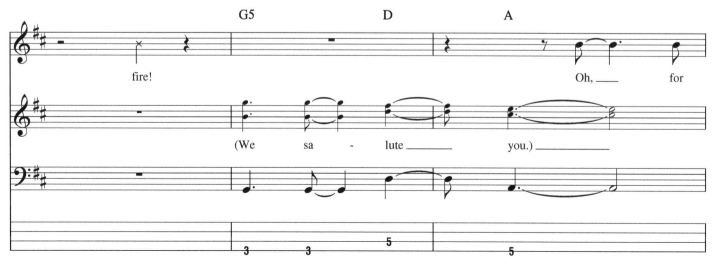

fire!

Oh, ___ for

(We sa - lute ___ you.) ___

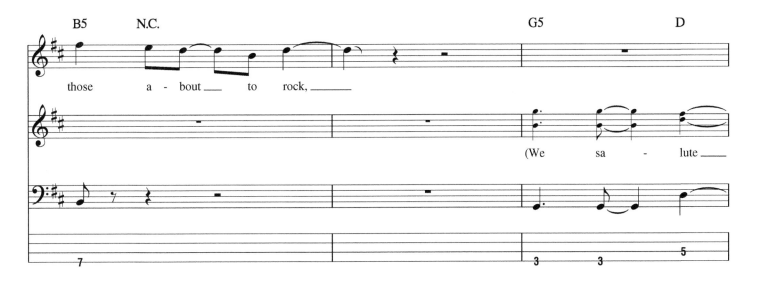

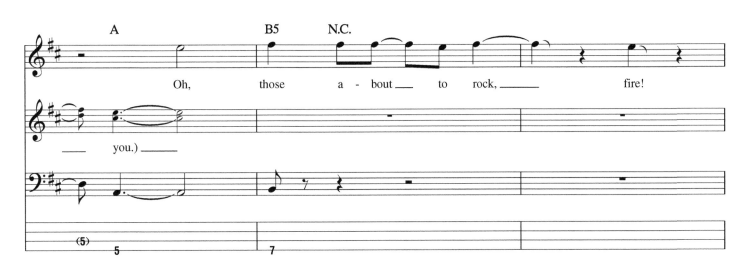

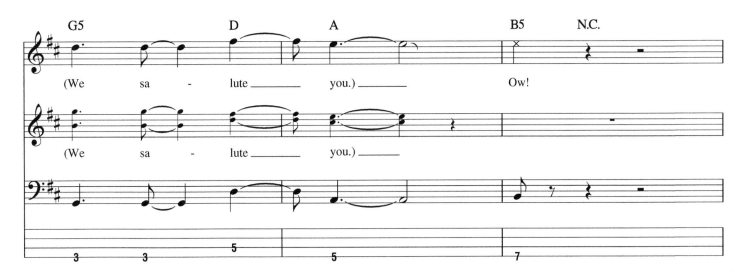

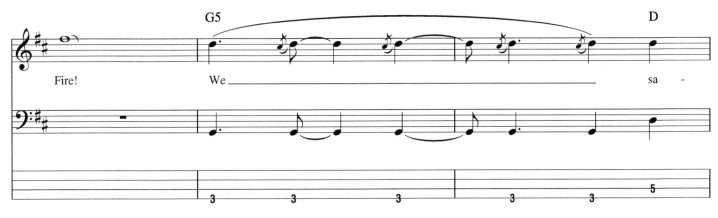

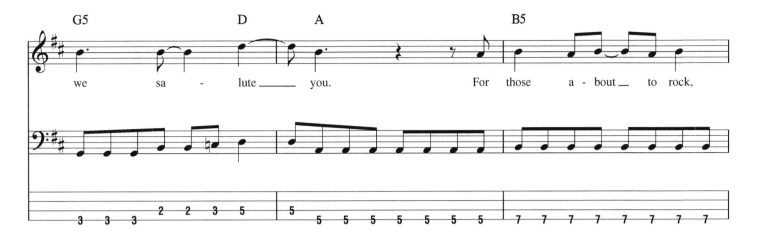

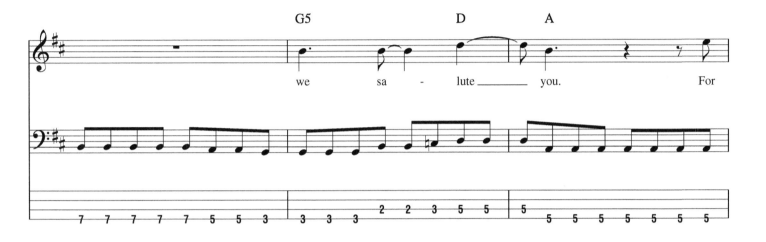

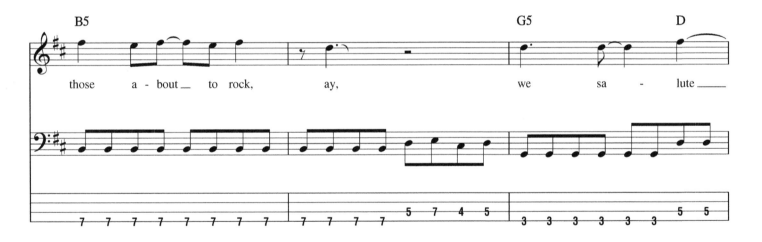

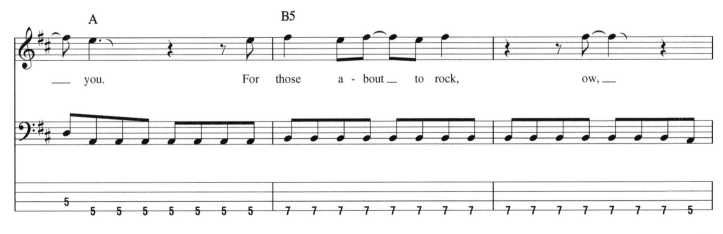

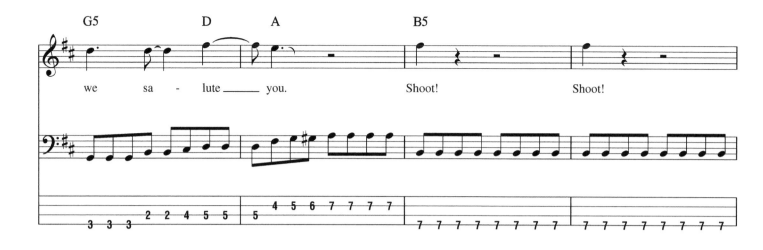

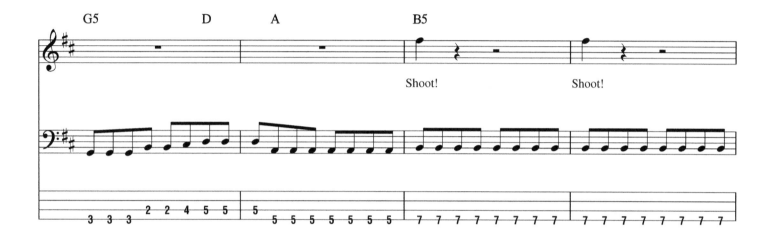

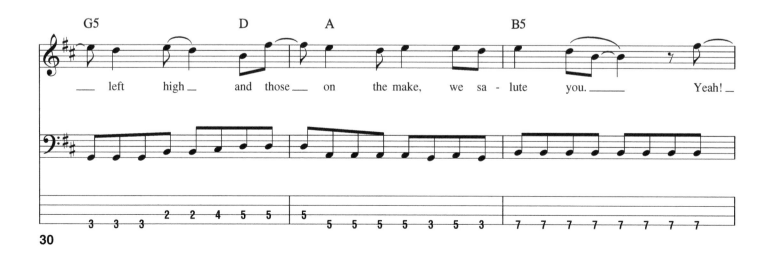

Additional Lyrics

2. We rock at dawn on the front line,
   Like a bolt right out of the blue.
   The sky's alight with the guitar bite.
   Heads will roll and rock tonight.

Girls Got Rhythm

Words and Music by Angus Young, Malcom Young and Bon Scott

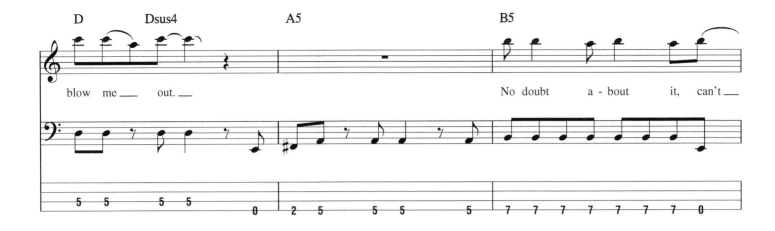

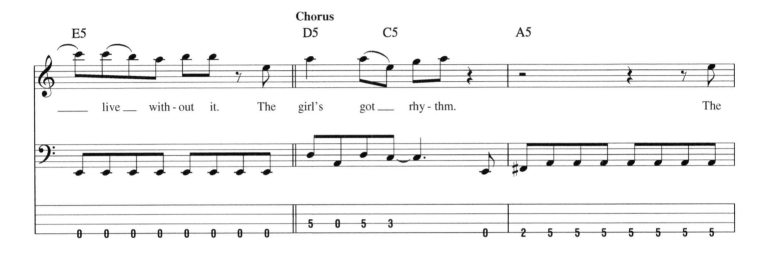

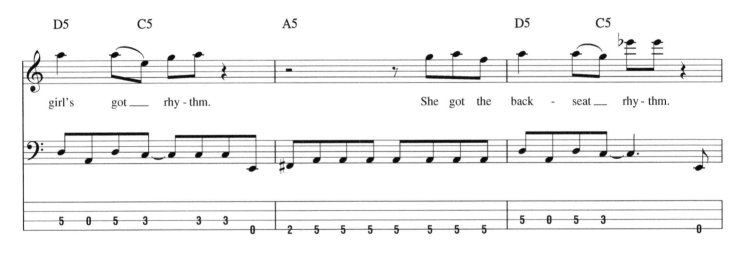

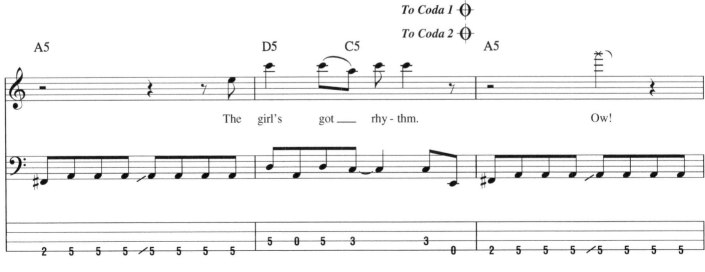

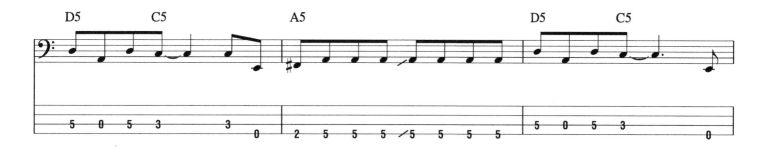

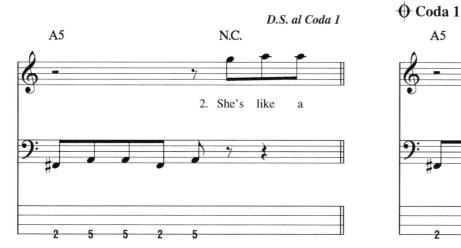

D.S. al Coda 1

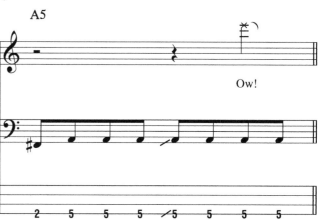

⊕ **Coda 1**

2. She's like a

Ow!

Guitar Solo

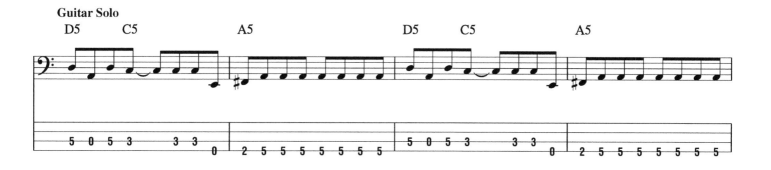

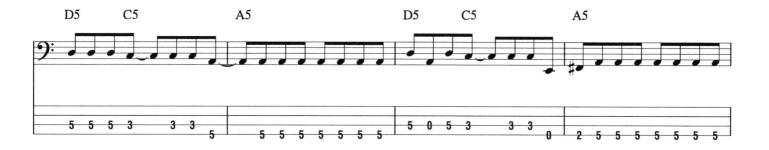

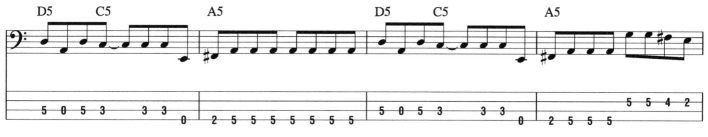

Additional Lyrics

2. She's like a lethal brand, too much for any man.
   She give me first degree, she really satisfy me.
   Love me till I'm legless, achin' and sore.
   Enough to stop a freight train or start the third world war.

Pre-Chorus 2. You know I'm losin' sleep, but I'm in too deep.
   Like a body need blood,
   No doubt about it, can't live without it.

Pre-Chorus 3. You know she move like sin, and when she let me in,
   It's like a liquid love.
   No doubt about it, can't live without it.

Hells Bells

Words and Music by Angus Young, Malcolm Young and Brian Johnson

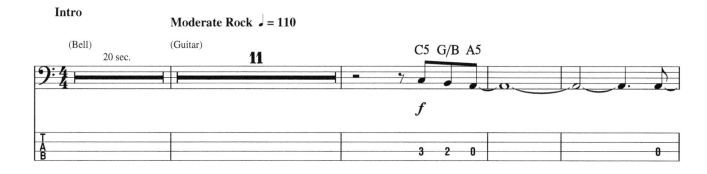

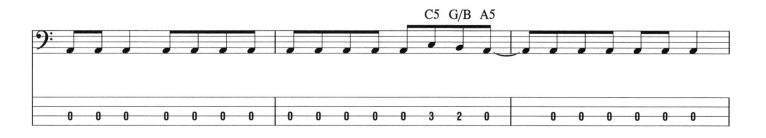

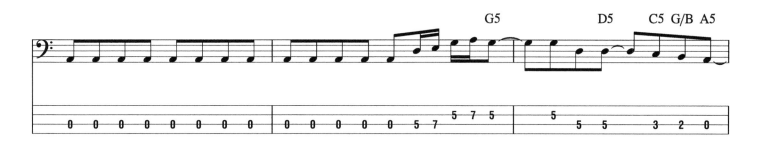

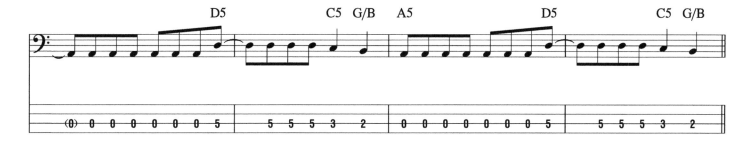

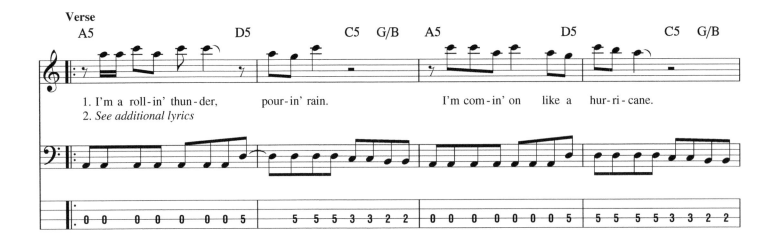

Verse

1. I'm a roll-in' thun-der, pour-in' rain. I'm com-in' on like a hur-ri-cane.
2. *See additional lyrics*

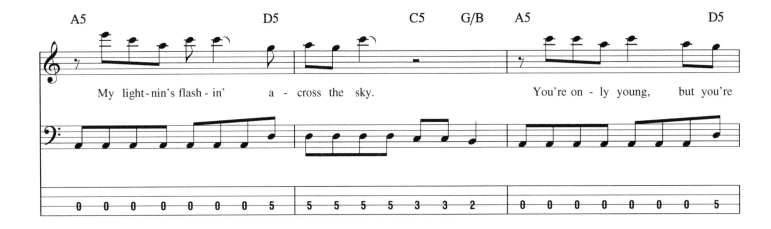

My light-nin's flash-in' a - cross the sky. You're on - ly young, but you're

Pre-Chorus

gon - na die. I _____ won't take no pris-on-ers, won't _____ spare no lives.

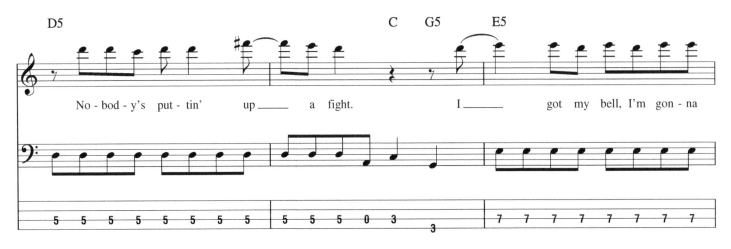

No - bod - y's put - tin' up _____ a fight. I _____ got my bell, I'm gon - na

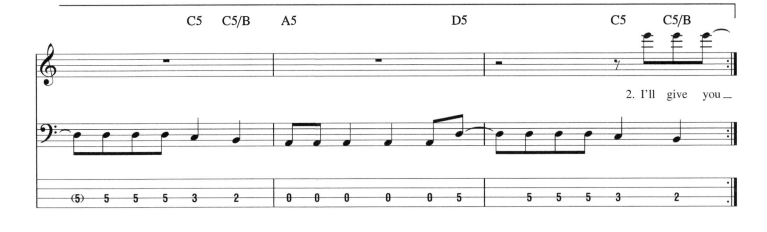

C5 C5/B A5   D5   C5 C5/B

2. I'll give you

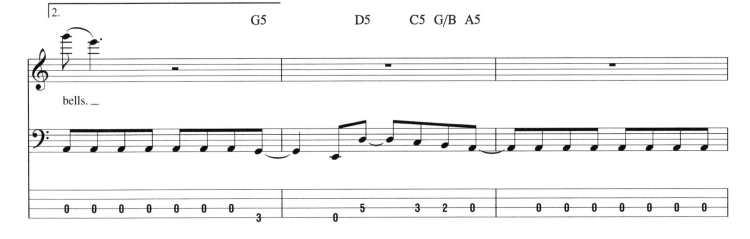

2.

G5   D5   C5 G/B A5

bells.

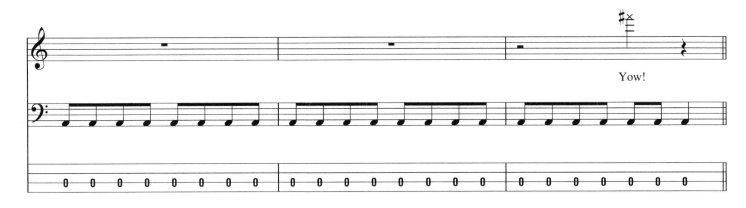

Yow!

Guitar Solo

A5 G5 A5   C5   D5   A5 G5 A5   C5   D5

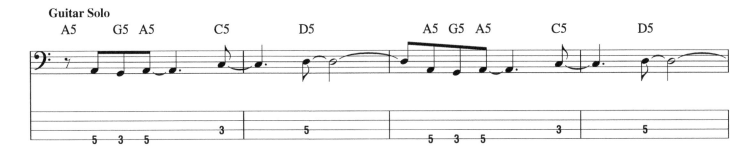

A5 G5 A5   C5   D5   A5 G5 A5   C5   D5

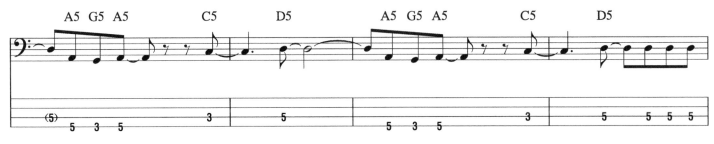

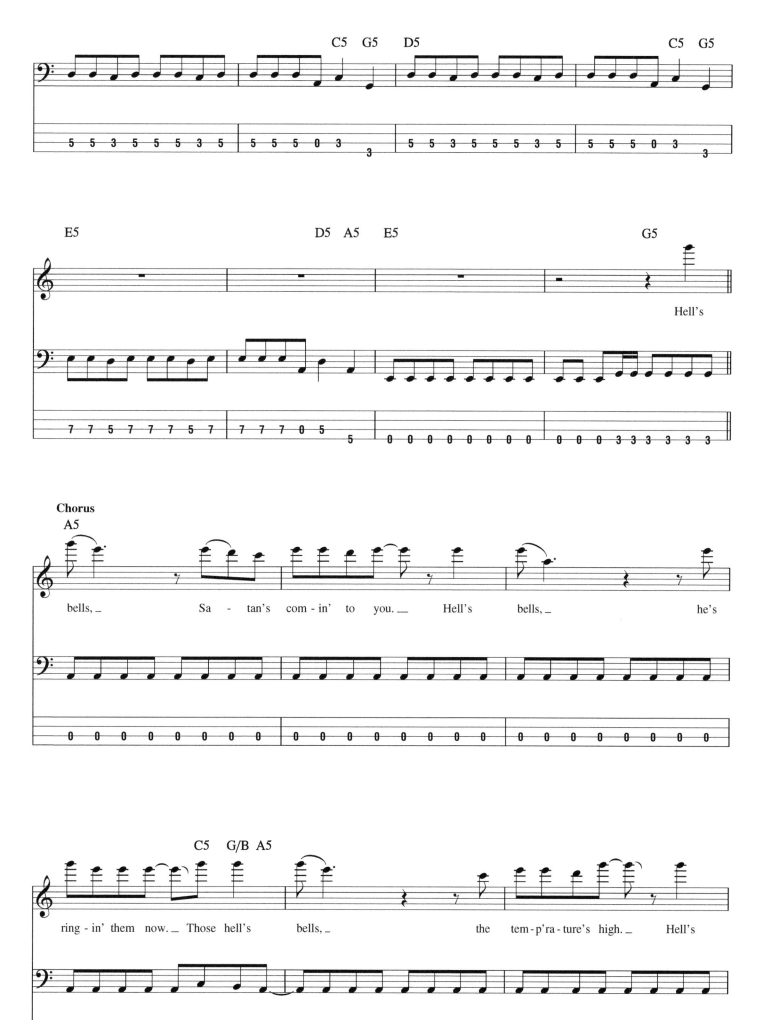

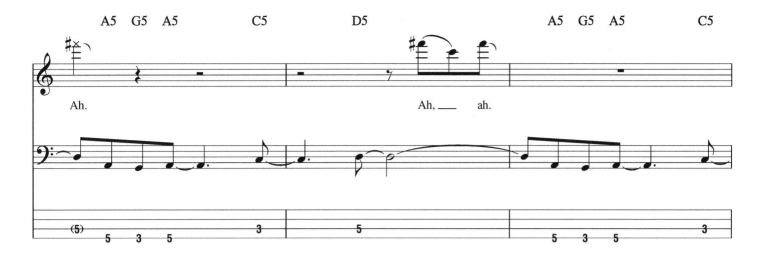

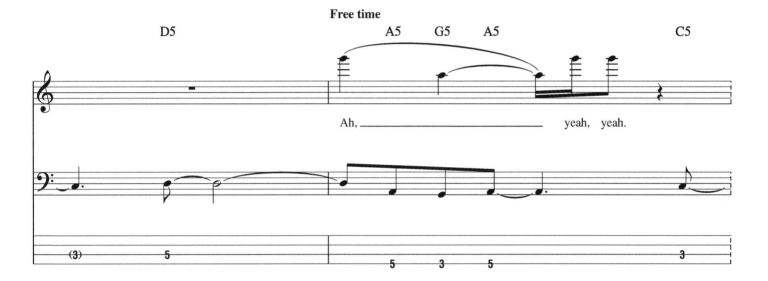

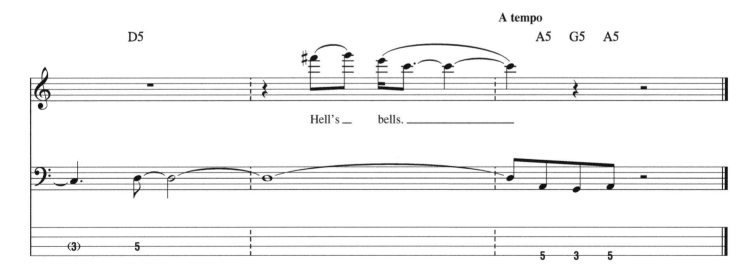

Additional Lyrics

2. I'll give you black sensations up and down your spine.
   If you're into evil, you're a friend of mine.
   See my white light flashin' as I split the night,
   'Cause if good's on the left, then I'm stickin' to the right.

Highway to Hell

Words and Music by Angus Young, Malcolm Young and Bon Scott

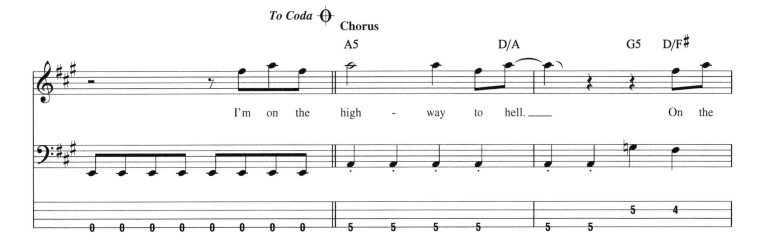

To Coda ⊕ **Chorus**

I'm on the high - way to hell. _____ On the

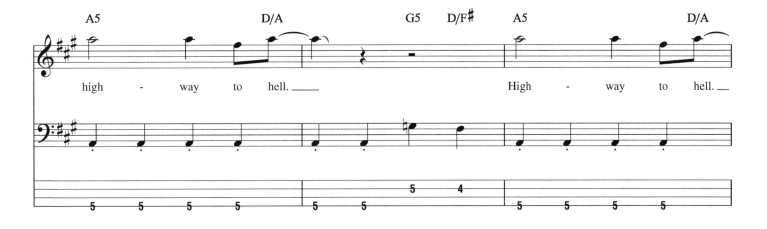

high - way to hell. _____ High - way to hell. _____

D.S. al Coda

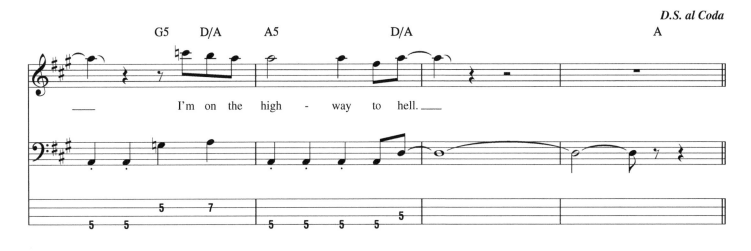

_____ I'm on the high - way to hell. _____

⊕ **Coda**

Chorus

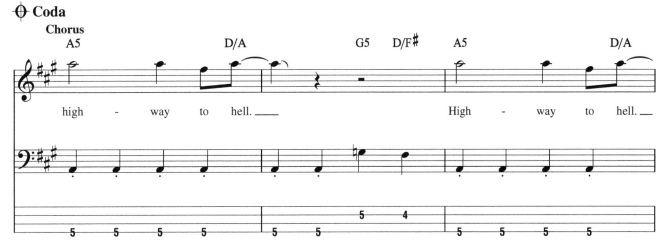

high - way to hell. _____ High - way to hell. _____

Additional Lyrics

2. No stop signs, speed limit, nobody's gonna slow me down.
   Like a wheel, gonna spin it, nobody's gonna mess me around.
   Hey Satan, pay'n' my dues, playin' in a rockin' band.
   Hey mama, look at me, I'm on my way to the promised land. Whoa!

T.N.T.

Words and Music by Angus Young, Malcolm Young and Bon Scott

Wom - en to ___ the left ___ of me, ___

and wom - en to the right. ___ Ain't got no gun, ___ ain't

got no knife. ___ Don't ___ you start no fight. ___

§ Chorus

'Cause I'm T. N. T. I'm dy - na - mite. ___

Verse

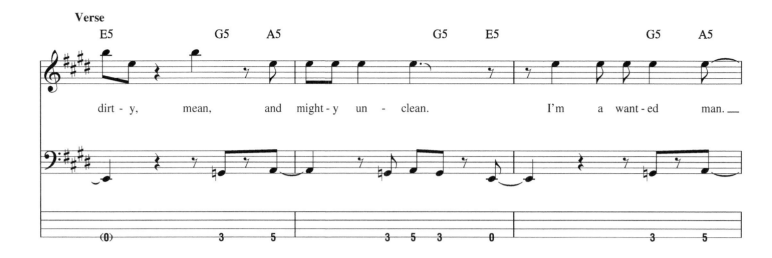

dirt - y, mean, and might - y un - clean. I'm a want - ed man. __

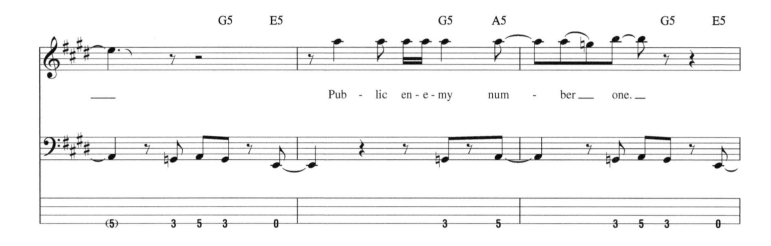

__ Pub - lic en - e - my num - ber __ one. __

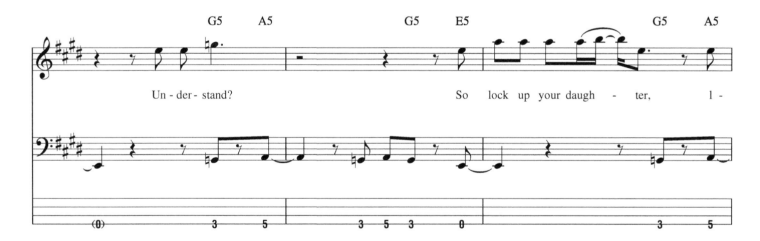

Un - der - stand? So lock up your daugh - ter, l -

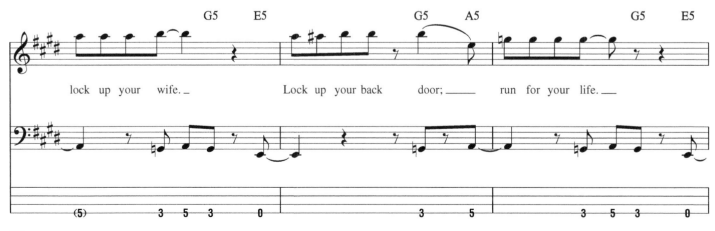

lock up your wife. _ Lock up your back door; ___ run for your life. __

The man is ____ back in town, ____ so don't you mess me 'round. ____

D.S. al Coda

____ 'Cause I'm

$\oplus$ **Coda**

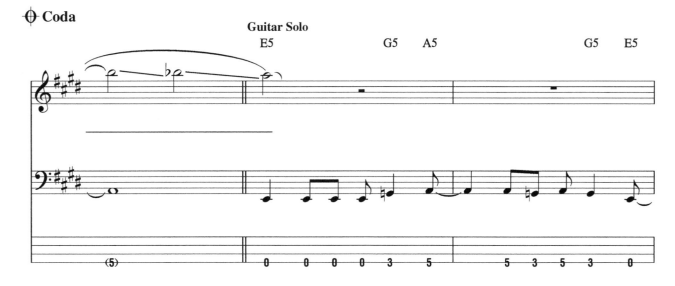

Guitar Solo

Bridge

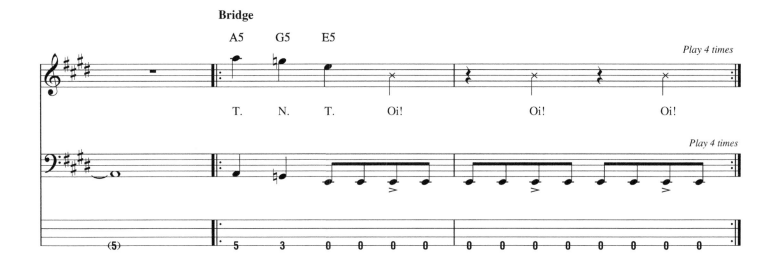

Chorus

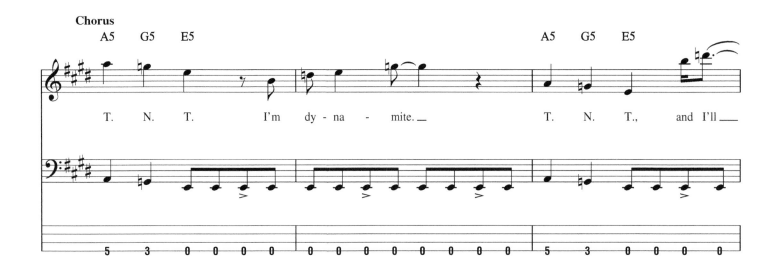

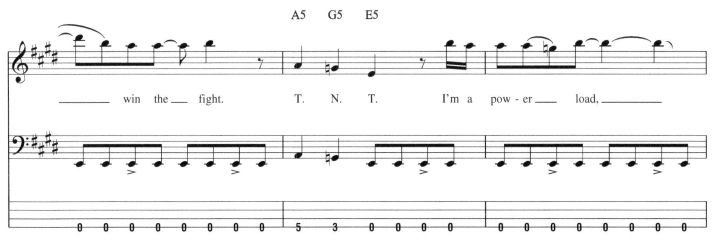

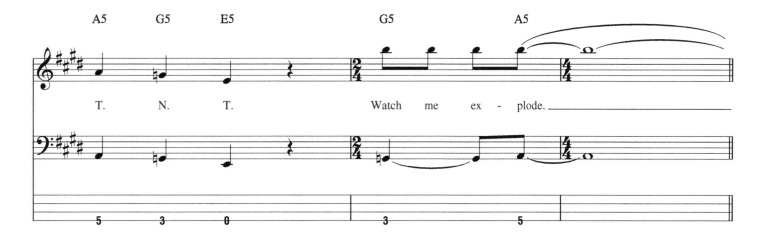

Outro

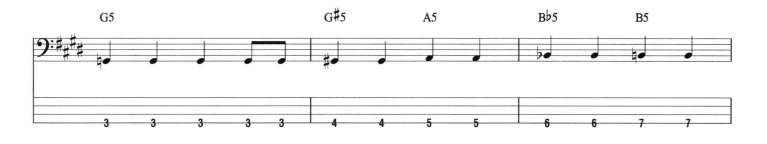

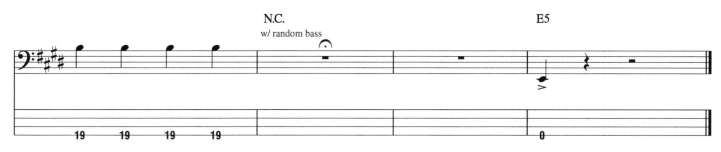

You Shook Me All Night Long

Words and Music by Angus Young, Malcolm Young and Brian Johnson

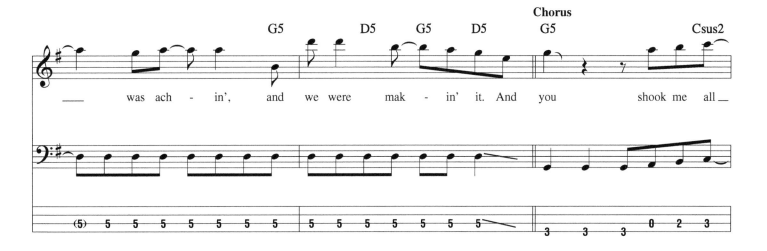

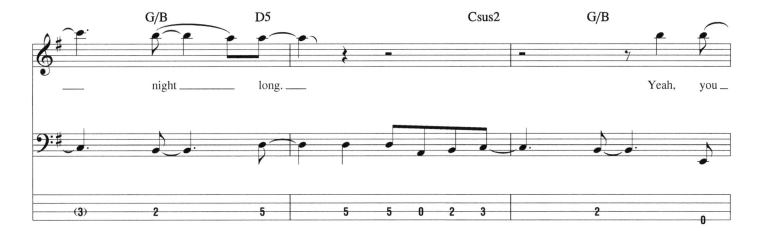

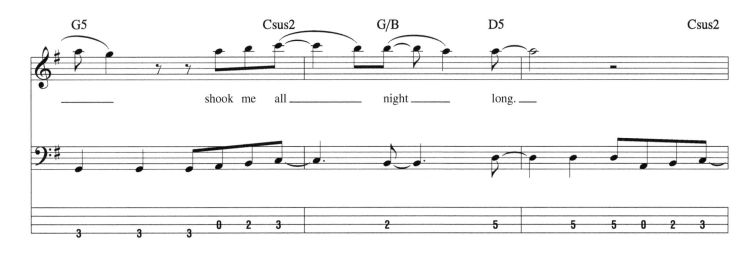

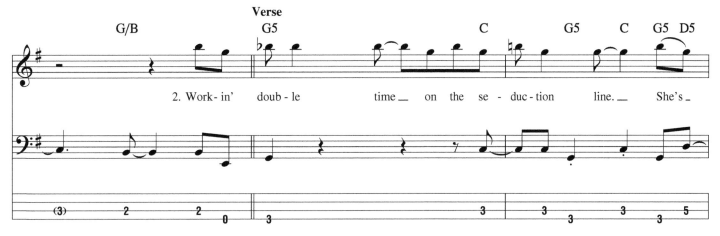

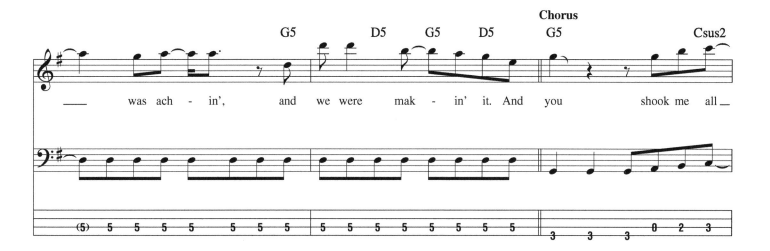

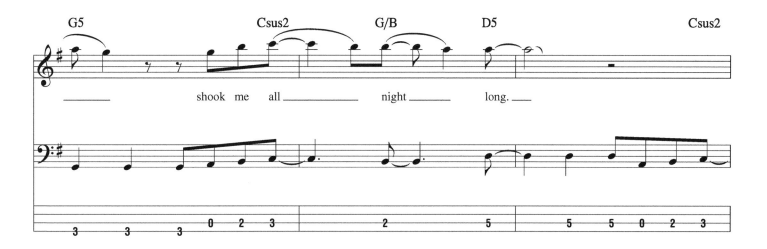

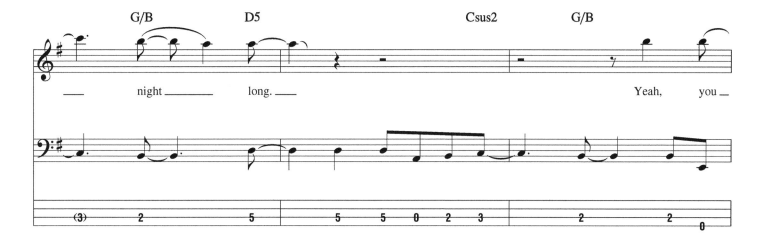

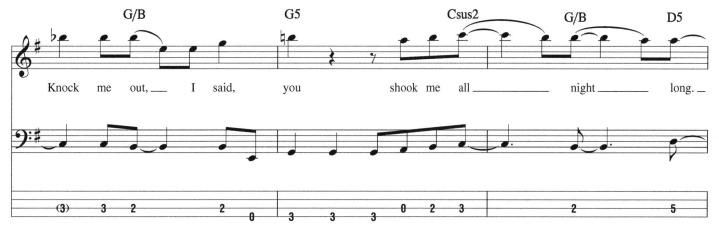

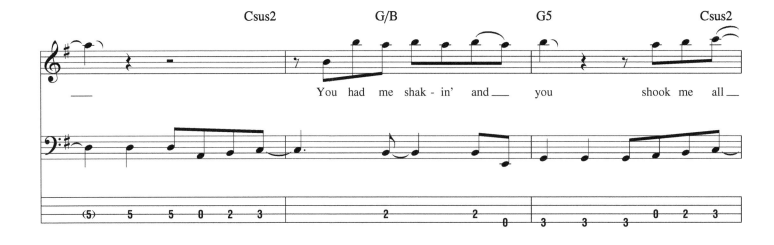

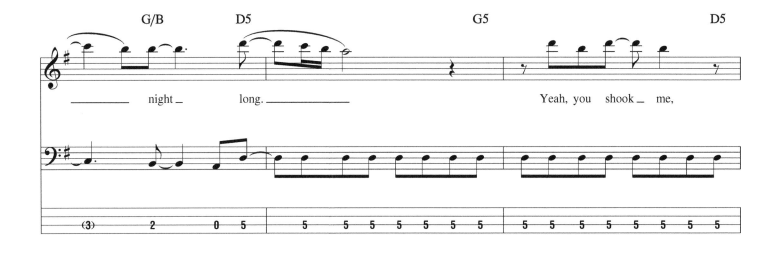

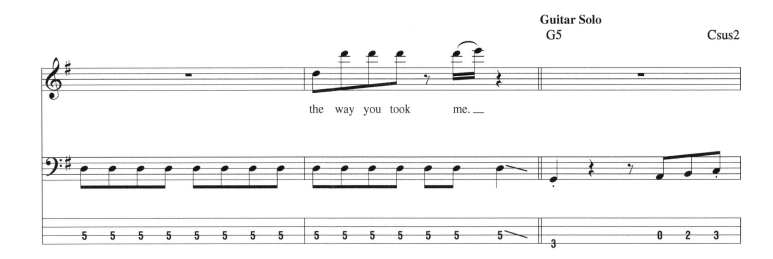

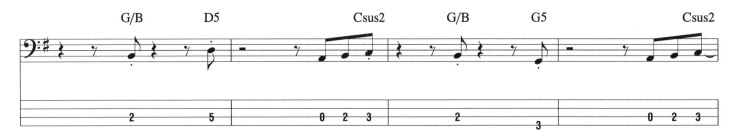

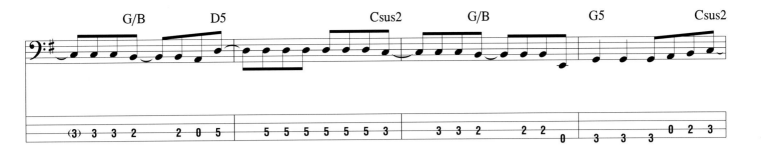

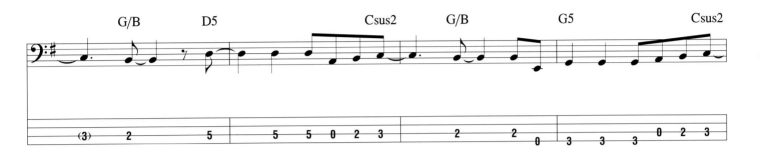

You real - ly took me, and

Outro-Chorus

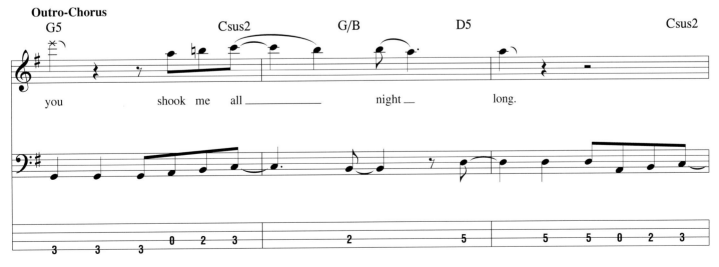

you   shook me   all _____   night _   long.

Ah, _____ you _____ shook me all _____ night _____

long. Yeah, _ yeah, _ you _____ shook me all _

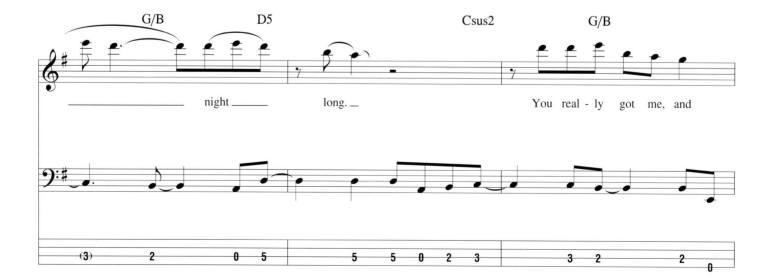

_____ night _____ long. _ You real-ly got me, and

you ____ shook me all _____ night __ long.

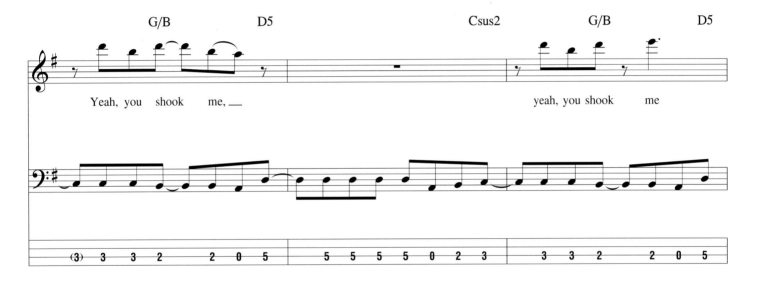

Yeah, you shook me, ____ yeah, you shook me

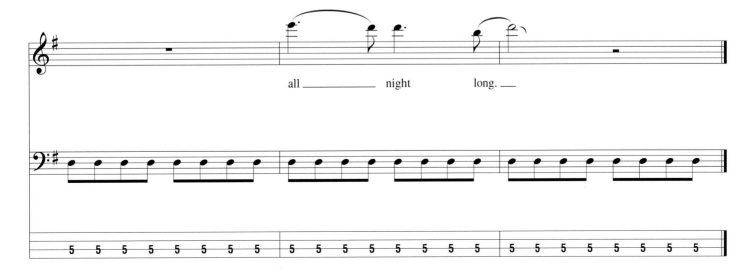

all _____ night long. ____

HAL·LEONARD®
BASS
PLAY-ALONG

The Bass Play-Along™ Series will help you play your favorite songs quickly and easily! Just follow the tab, listen to the audio to hear how the bass should sound, and then play-along using the separate backing tracks. The melody and lyrics are also included in the book in case you want to sing, or to simply help you follow along. The audio files are enhanced so you can adjust the recording to any tempo without changing pitch!

1. Rock
00699674 Book/Online Audio $16.99
2. R&B
00699675 Book/Online Audio $15.99
3. Pop/Rock
00699677 Book/Online Audio $16.99
4. '90s Rock
00699677 Book/Online Audio $16.99
5. Funk
00699680 Book/Online Audio.....................$16.99
6. Classic Rock
00699678 Book/Online Audio $17.99
8. Punk Rock
00699813 Book/CD Pack $12.95
9. Blues
00699817 Book/Online Audio.....................$16.99
10. Jimi Hendrix – Smash Hits
00699815 Book/Online Audio......................$17.99
11. Country
00699818 Book/CD Pack $12.95
12. Punk Classics
00699814 Book/CD Pack $12.99
13. The Beatles
00275504 Book/Online Audio $16.99
14. Modern Rock
00699821 Book/CD Pack.........................$14.99
15. Mainstream Rock
00699822 Book/CD Pack..........................$14.99
16. '80s Metal
00699825 Book/CD Pack..........................$16.99
17. Pop Metal
00699826 Book/CD Pack..........................$14.99
18. Blues Rock
00699828 Book/CD Pack..........................$16.99
19. Steely Dan
00700203 Book/Online Audio $16.99
20. The Police
00700270 Book/Online Audio $19.99
21. Metallica: 1983-1988
00234338 Book/Online Audio $19.99
22. Metallica: 1991-2016
00234339 Book/Online Audio $19.99

23. Pink Floyd – Dark Side of The Moon
00700847 Book/Online Audio $15.99
24. Weezer
00700960 Book/CD Pack..........................$14.99
25. Nirvana
00701047 Book/Online Audio $17.99
26. Black Sabbath
00701180 Book/Online Audio $16.99
27. Kiss
00701181 Book/Online Audio......................$16.99
28. The Who
00701182 Book/Online Audio $19.99
29. Eric Clapton
00701183 Book/Online Audio $15.99
30. Early Rock
00701184 Book/CD Pack..........................$15.99
31. The 1970s
00701185 Book/CD Pack..........................$14.99
32. Cover Band Hits
00211598 Book/Online Audio $16.99
33. Christmas Hits
00701197 Book/CD Pack $12.99
34. Easy Songs
00701480 Book/Online Audio.....................$16.99
35. Bob Marley
00701702 Book/Online Audio $17.99
36. Aerosmith
00701886 Book/CD Pack..........................$14.99
37. Modern Worship
00701920 Book/Online Audio $17.99
38. Avenged Sevenfold
00702386 Book/CD Pack...........................$16.99
39. Queen
00702387 Book/Online Audio $16.99

40. AC/DC
14041594 Book/Online Audio $16.99
41. U2
00702582 Book/Online Audio $16.99
42. Red Hot Chili Peppers
00702991 Book/Online Audio.....................$19.99
43. Paul McCartney
00703079 Book/Online Audio $17.99
44. Megadeth
00703080 Book/CD Pack $16.99
45. Slipknot
00703201 Book/CD Pack $16.99
46. Best Bass Lines Ever
00103359 Book/Online Audio......................$19.99
47. Dream Theater
00111940 Book/Online Audio $24.99
48. James Brown
00117421 Book/CD Pack..........................$16.99
49. Eagles
00119936 Book/Online Audio $17.99
50. Jaco Pastorius
00128407 Book/Online Audio......................$17.99
51. Stevie Ray Vaughan
00146154 Book/CD Pack $16.99
52. Cream
00146159 Book/Online Audio $17.99
56. Bob Seger
00275503 Book/Online Audio $16.99
57. Iron Maiden
00278398 Book/Online Audio $17.99
58. Southern Rock
00278436 Book/Online Audio $17.99

HAL·LEONARD®

Prices, contents, and availability subject to change without notice.

Visit Hal Leonard Online at www.halleonard.com

0920
334